A GIRL'S GATEWAY TO WOMANHOOD

A RITE OF PASSAGE GUIDEBOOK

PART 1
FOR GIRLS

BY

FREDERICA CHAPMAN

"You need to claim the events of your life
to make your life yours."
Anne-Wilson Schaef

authorHOUSE®

AuthorHouse™
1663 Liberty Drive, Suite 200
Bloomington, IN 47403
www.authorhouse.com
Phone: 1-800-839-8640

First published by AuthorHouse 4/17/2008

ISBN: 978-1-4343-4370-3 (sc)

Printed in the United States of America
Bloomington, Indiana

This book is printed on acid-free paper.

For my children
Becca, Kate, Eben, Peter, Hilary
and for girls everywhere

THANK YOU

To the wonderful women of *Theatre For The Earth* for their creative assistance in developing this work: Mary Blum, Hilary Chapman, Eva Fitzgerald, Sarah Schneider, and Janice Cox. To Jane Burdick and Lisa Hicks for leading the way in mentoring my daughter. Many thanks to Bonnie Walstrom for her enthusiasm in the long editing process. Lastly, warm thanks to Heather Alexander for her lovely graphics, and to Moosey, at Moosey's Country Garden, New Zealand, for her perfectly beautiful "Pink Rose Fairy" photo generously given for our cover.

TABLE OF CONTENTS

And the Grandmother said,

   "Child of mine, Child of the heart of the world, Listen,
   Listen to your own heart, to its rhythm, to its truth.

   Your life is a story, a beautiful story in the making.
Every day, every page, you write, you choose, you decide
   How it will be – the words, the pictures, the colors.

   How your story will be, so that when it is finished,
      And when you read the whole thing through,
You will be satisfied. You will know that all has been said.
You will know that your story holds the true expression
                of who you really are...

   Child of mine, listen to your own true heart."

And since the Grandmother had lived a very long time, the
girl believed that what she said was so...

Dear Girls,

All my life I have been following girls' and women's life stories. As a therapist, I've listened to hundreds of stories from girls, and from young and older women. As a theatre director, I've written and performed fairy tales about girls and women. What I've learned is that our stories (yours and mine) can be inspiring and helpful to others. I've also learned that we are making-up our life stories as we go, and therefore, we have choices about them. Our stories have all sorts of possibilities, if we take the time to think about them. When we do, then we can make positive choices for ourselves.

Perhaps your mother or your grandmother has given this book to you, and perhaps, like most girls your age, you feel less like doing what your mother, or grandmother wants you to do, and more like doing what you, and your friends want to do. Like most girls, you may be pulling away from your older generations to do things differently and more independently. Like most girls, you are probably experiencing many big changes. In fact, you are undoubtedly moving through one of the biggest changes of your life – you are moving from your childhood into young womanhood!

In this book, I suggest that you celebrate the changes you are making, and that you make this celebration more important than a Birthday Party. I suggest that you light candles and make wishes within a circle of your girlfriends, your relatives, and women friends to mark your entrance into this whole new chapter of your life story. I suggest that you call it a "Gateway" celebration, since a gateway provides a good image for the change that is occurring – but, of course, what you choose to call it is up to you. All you will need to create a successful Gateway Celebration is: a sense of imagination, someone to help you make an initial plan (mother, father, or if they are absent, a guardian or older friend), mentors, a group of women and girls, and a spirit of adventure.

I hope that you will take advantage of what my generation of women has learned about the strength that is available to us from circles of support. Many of us have learned this in our later years. I hope you will get the information you need earlier in your lives, and I hope you will allow us older women to welcome you in, as you begin your journeys into womanhood.

You, alone, have to decide whether a Gateway celebration is worthwhile for you, but it is my hope that each of you will create a personal and wonderful Gateway celebration.

I hope that by making a celebration to mark this passage into womanhood, many things will come about: you will come to know yourselves better, you will believe (without doubt) in your own goodness and worth, and you will deepen your connection to your girlfriends and to older women. Also, as you work with your mentors, you will develop the courage to discover your inner gifts and be willing to share them with others.

The gifts that each of you brings are important for you to offer, and they are important for your community to receive. As a girl soon-to-be-a-woman in a world that (we hope) offers more choices for our gender, we older women welcome you for who you are and for what you bring. We wish you the very best.

P.S.
If the Gateway Ceremony doesn't fit your style, then I encourage you to find another way to mark this new chapter of your life. Take the time to consider your story thus far, and to make wishes for your future. If you have felt rejected or misunderstood, let this be a time for healing and for setting a positive course for your life. It's up to you to make your story your very own.

Sincerely,

Frederica

You Are Unique

"There is a vitality, a life force,
an energy, a quickening,
that is translated through you into action,
and because there is only one of you in all time,
the expression is unique.
And if you block it, it will never exist
through any other medium and will be lost."
Martha Graham, dancer/choreographer

You are not alone in coming into womanhood. Millions of girls are your age now, millions have been your age before, and millions will be your age in the future. Yet there is no one like you now, nor will there ever be anyone like you... Ever. There is no one who has lived your set of experiences to this date, nor will there ever be. It's really very wonderful. You are incomparable. You are yourself alone, and you have everything you need to be fully you. Can you feel it? When you feel how unique you are, you may also begin to feel a question arising that might go something like this: "So

I am unique – what am I going to do with all this uniqueness?"

If you look at your life story as it "reads" so far, what does it seem to be saying about who you are? Can you list your particular interests and skills – things that you have felt (maybe privately) very good about, things that you love?

Can you remember when you've felt that some sport, artform, or area of study was "yours"? Can you recall the compliments you've received about who you are, or what you've done? Can you choose what it is about yourself becoming a woman that you want to celebrate?

Could you appreciate all that is happening, and could you create a celebration exactly because what is happening is a big event in your life? Could you choose to be aware of the feelings surrounding you at this time, meet those feelings (such as sadness, elation, fear, excitement, uncertainty, etc.), and move through them with awareness, even excitement?

Life changes generally happen subtly, and the change called adolescence is no exception. You may be vaguely aware of leaving one way of being, and entering a new one. You are probably feeling less like a child, (though of course you will always keep who you have been as a child inside you). You may or may not have started your menstrual periods, but your body may be outwardly changing. You may already be taking on new responsibilities, and experiencing your friends, family, and schoolwork in new ways. These changes may make you feel sad, alone, or even frightened – so much is happening.

You may be thinking, "Why would anyone necessarily want to be aware? Why would anyone choose to feel a feeling, especially if the feeling is uncomfortable?" It is pretty simple really – the more you know about your inner situation (including your feelings), and your outer situation, the more information you will have available to make the best possible choices for yourself.

What I am suggesting to you is not easy. In the short run, it might seem easier to avoid your feelings, but by doing so, you will actually make it harder for yourself. Remember, even under the best of circumstances, adolescence is a transitional time, and transitions usually bring disruption, and uncertainty. As a friend of mine has reminded me, "the way *out* of a situation is always *through*." When you move through your feelings, when you sort things out, your story and your reason to celebrate will become clearer to you.

CELEBRATING YOUR STORY

"That which is not celebrated, that which is not ritualized goes unnoticed...The smallest events can be made into great moments of our lives by taking the time to celebrate them."

Zou Zsanna E. Budapest, spiritual leader, author

Our society comprises people from many different cultures. Each of these cultures has different rituals for celebrating life passages. Ancient cultures have used rites of passage for girls and for boys for thousands of years. The important concept is that each young person has a "bridge" to cross, or a "gateway" to enter to represent the passage to be made from childhood into adulthood. It is important that the new and more responsible status is established for the young person and for the community.

You might be interested to know, that in parts of Africa, South America, and in some Native American communities, when girls begin menstruation, they are secluded and taught the ways of womanhood by the older females in their community. Eshira girls of Gabon, Africa paint their faces with powdered clay, Apache girls are sprinkled with yellow cattail pollen, and Lesse girls in Zaire paint white designs on their faces. Ritual clothing, symbolic body art, chant, song, and formalized instruction on the responsibilities of sexual maturity and motherhood mark these passages of girls in many non-industrialized countries. In Western society (such as America) we have forgotten the importance of these passages.

Your culture may have a specified ritual for entering adolescence, or not. What I am suggesting in the Gateway celebration is: 1. that you set aside the time to make the celebration, and 2. that you use the Gateway celebration on its own, or that you blend it with any other form that suits you and your family. Anything that you can imagine to create is possible – all the better when you make it your own.

Imagining the Possibilities

"By replacing 'No way!' with 'Maybe,'
we open the door to mystery and to magic."
Julia Cameron, artist, teacher, author

Sometimes, when I am thinking hard about something that I want to have happen, or about a question that I have, I try to forget about it, and an answer comes "out of the blue". After I have thought and thought, I go for a walk, or do something else that busies my mind, and suddenly, the answer pops into my head – I know exactly what I need to know! We all have instinctive knowing, or intuition, but we must open up to "hearing" it, or to sensing it. Try this for yourself!

As you begin to imagine how you want your celebration to be, you set creativity into motion. The celebration will seem to have a life of its own. Keep a watchful eye and a listening ear for interesting ideas – ideas you might not have imagined at first. Keep a notebook (particularly by your bedside) to jot down ideas that spontaneously come to you. They might come from your own thoughts and dreams, or they might come from nature, or from other people. You might want to share what you are imagining with a parent, teacher, or a friend. It is a wonderful time to reinforce your relationship with an important adult in your life, and since you will need help with your plans, sharing your ideas will move things along.

An important part of preparing for your celebration will be to imagine a personal challenge that you will work to accomplish in time to present at your celebration. This accomplishment will demonstrate to your community of girls and women your readiness for the next chapter of your life. What could you accomplish and present at your celebration to demonstrate your focus and your ability? What inner gifts or talents do you have to bring?

Each person has many possibilities, but you must base the challenge on what it is *you love to do*, and then challenge yourself to go beyond what you have achieved so far.

For example:
* If you are a music student, and this is something you love, you could choose to perform something meaningful to you, something that is beyond your current skill. Or you could compose a new work to perform at your celebration.
* If you like working with paint or clay, you could create something that represents the new images

and ideas that you are having about yourself as a woman.

* If you like to swim, you could arrange to have your celebration at a pool or lake, and swim a distance within a designated time.

* If you like to read or to write, you could present some readings that relate to your becoming a woman, or you could write a story or some poetry to present.

There are as many ideas as there are girls to do them! You may choose to focus on two things that you love; for example, if you love to ride your bicycle, and if you love to sing, find something to sing which expresses your feeling about biking and being outdoors. You could display your pottery pieces and also present a dance if these are your interests.

Are you getting the idea? As you are imagining what you could do, you may also be discovering more of what it is you like. Remember, there is no comparison to be made with others, since you are uniquely yourself, and as such, a precious gift to us all.

Your Woman's Circle

"Mother-daughter, sister-sister, grandmother-
granddaughter, kinships reach backward and forward
in an unbroken line of generational connectedness."
Adrienne Rich, feminist writer

Since this is a celebration of your identity as an emerging woman, it is appropriate that you gather a circle of girls and women into which you will make an entrance, and out of which you will emerge as a newly recognized young woman. Your mother, aunts, grandmothers, sisters, and girlfriends probably comprise your present community of women. For your celebration, you will be bringing together those whom you care about and love, and those who love you. You will be choosing the friends and the older women to be in you circle. You will be confirming your own system of support.

The women (particularly your mentors) will play the larger part in guiding you, and in seeing you through the challenge which you have set for yourself. These are the women who will welcome you into womanhood. Hopefully, you will find support from the males in your life too. Ask yourself if it seems important to mark your passage in a separate event with them.

CHOOSING YOUR MENTORS

"How might your life have been different,
if there had been a place for you, a place of women?
... somewhat older, already initiated—
if the women had helped you draw
your thoughts and feelings together
and to weigh them...so that you could come
to a clearer knowing of what your life was about."

Judith Duerk, author and workshop leader

These words were written with women of my generation in mind. It is because of such women as Judith Duerk that the women of my generation are positioning themselves to be mentors for your generation. It is your task to find us, and I believe that you will easily find us, for we are all around you.

Mentors for a Gateway Ceremony will be one or two women who:
* are important to you as your friends, or your personal teachers, and with whom you would like to spend more time

* are skilled in your areas of interest (to guide you in preparing your challenge)
* will help and support you as you plan and accomplish your challenge, and as you create your celebration
* have time (over a two-three month period) and who live near enough to meet with you weekly
* your parents approve of

Your job with your mentors is:
* to come up with your own ideas for your challenge and for your celebration, and to share these ideas with them
* to listen and to learn
* to set the meetings with your mentors and to ask for the help you need from them
* to share any confusion or difficulty you have during the time you are accomplishing your challenge

Think of two (or, perhaps three) women you like. For example, your mentor could be a coach, a teacher, a friend's mother, or someone with whom you feel friendly.

Think of women who could guide you in your particular area of focus.

Do you think your parents would feel comfortable with the women you are suggesting as your mentors? Your parents' input is important because they have nourished and cared for you in the past. They still care for you, and they want to know and to trust those who will be helping and guiding you. Can you work together with your parents (or guardians) on this? Can you respect each other's ideas and come to a mutually agreeable decision? As you change, your family will be changing as well. As you establish yourself as more of an adult, your relationship with your parents and siblings will change. This is natural. This is a time to establish new boundaries and new connections with each other. It could be a time for deepening respect and mutual support. You could participate in making it so.

Setting Your Date

"It's time to get started.
It's time to wake-up.
Don't wait another minute.
Claim your heart and claim your glory.
You have all you need...
The new world will seem
like nothing you have seen before.
It will be reborn like you.
It will shine like you.
It will smile like you.
It will feel like home."

Marianne Williamson, author, lecturer

Setting the date establishes your commitment. It's like saying, "on this date I expect all aspects of my celebration to be ready." From my experience, it works like this: when you make a future date for something, events come together for you, people appear and ideas emerge, seemingly, once again, "out of the blue". Setting the date puts change into motion and calls the pieces together.

With your date set, you have a target to aim for. You can schedule time to meet with your mentors, and you can make time to meet the challenge you have set. A time frame allows thoughts and feelings to come to the surface, so you can resolve them. It allows you to get used to the idea of becoming more adult, and integrate your changes, at the same time that others are accepting them too. This designated period could be thought of as your "seclusion" – not a physical seclusion as for the tribal girls of Africa, South or North America, but a personal seclusion in which you will be taking more time with yourself and with the process of preparation (you can use the pages in the back of this book as a journal).

On what factors will you base the setting of this date? You may feel that you want to wait until your menstrual periods come before setting a date, or you could decide that your sense of knowing will tell you what is right. Here are some ideas to consider:

* Is there a day that has special meaning to you, such as your Birthday?

* When will your parent and your mentors be available?

* Which girls and women do you absolutely have to have present at your celebration and when will they be available?

* When will the chosen facility/location be available for your celebration?

Your Location

"I saw the moon through the branches of the hazel tree
and the outline of the hill springing behind it,
and I knew that this was the place I should be."
Monica Furlong, author of novels and biographies

Your gateway celebration marks your entrance into the world that is beyond your family home. For this reason, it could be significant to locate this event away from the home in which you may be perceived as a child. Or, for you, it may be just the thing to have your celebration in your home, and make your Gateway a walk out through the front door of your house to symbolize going into the world.

Here are some things to consider regarding the location:

*   Will you be comfortable meeting your challenge in this location?

*   Do you get a good feeling from being in this place?

* Will it be easily accessible to friends and family?
* Can food be served easily?

Your Invitation

"When I looked at myself in the big bronze mirror,
I saw how grown-up I had become – very different
from the child who had sought her reflection there."
Monica Furlong, author

What you send out to your chosen circle of girls and women makes the initial statement of how you see yourself, and how you want people to see you. An image on an invitation engages others in the imagining of what you are doing. Be creative so that your invitation truly represents you. You could use a photo or drawing of yourself engaging in your chosen activity. As with all aspects of your celebration, I encourage you to take the time to think about what you want.

Here are some things to consider:
*   Select or draw an image that seems just right to describe your becoming a woman.
*   Think about what color you like, and how you want it to look on the page.

* What would inspire you to want to go to a friend's celebration?

Here is an example:

Please join us for
(your name)'s Party
To celebrate her passage into womanhood
(image here)
Date, Time and Location
(your name) will present_____that she has prepared.
A circle will form to offer gifts and blessings,
followed by dinner and dessert.
R.S.V.P to_____
(your mother's name and phone, or whoever is
coordinating the party).

Words of advice:
* Be fairly general about stating what you will be presenting (creative projects sometimes surprise you, and evolve into something different than you had intended)

* Be liberal in the number you invite (for one reason or another, some will not be able to attend)

* Send your invitations at least three weeks before the date (you could even send a "save the date" postcard 2 months before to assure a better attendance)

Meeting the Challenge

"Risk! Risk anything!
Care no more for the opinions of others, for those voices.
Do the hardest thing on earth for you.
Act for yourself.
Face the truth."
Katherine Mansfield, early 20th century author

Especially, "risk" counteracting *any inner voice* that might prevent you from succeeding at what you decide you want to do for your challenge. Together with your mentors, you will be establishing a realistic challenge that you will strive to meet before the date of your celebration. The purpose of the challenge is to help you know and appreciate yourself better, to develop your gifts further, and to present them to your circle. The challenge you set ought to be pleasurable, because it is something that you are drawn to, something that you love to do. No one is imposing this on you. This is a challenge you have chosen for yourself.

Do you know yourself well enough to recognize that you usually procrastinate, work too hard, or spend time worrying over a project? Here are some ideas for meeting your challenge:

* Work with your mentors on the pace of your tasks. Set interim target dates for having parts of your challenge accomplished. Be forgiving of yourself if you need more input or time.

* Do something (even one little thing) toward your challenge every day to keep the process alive and growing.

* Be open to creative impulses and spontaneity – if a new idea comes to you, be willing to consider it and let yourself explore this new idea.

* Observe whether you're having fun with this, or not. If not, then make adjustments so that it becomes fun.

* Keep in mind that this is about you, and about what you love to do.

* Seek out your mentors. Call them. Arrange meetings (either established weekly meetings or spontaneous ones, depending on your needs and theirs).

* Ask questions.

* Plan that you will be calm and prepared when your celebration day comes.

Naturally, the more you invest in your challenge, the more rewarding it will be.

YOUR CELEBRATION

"Gwenhwyfar felt that her whole body and heart were made of
pure joy.
She had not been as happy as this since she was a little child."
Marion Zimmer Bradley, author

While you are still working on your challenge, you will
be putting your joyful imagination to work as well.
Your playful self can go into action with ideas for the
actual celebration.

Your celebration will have a unique character because
you are unique. Let it be a reflection of you. There
are certainly many things to think about: guests, place,
food, the ritual, the order of events, and what you
will present. Perhaps your mother will work out the
details of the celebration, and you will focus more
on your presentation with your mentors, or you may
want to work with them all on certain aspects of the
whole celebration. A sister, aunt or friend may want to
participate in some part as well. While the old saying,

"Many hands make light work" applies to creating a celebration, I recommend that one person be in charge of coordinating the overall event. However it works best in your situation, be willing to share your ideas and be willing to listen to others' ideas.

Food is a natural and wholesome addition to celebrations. As a symbol, it represents the "taking in" of the event. If food is to be included in your celebration, here are some options:

*   The event could be a general "potluck"with your guests bringing their specialties, or requested dishes

*   You could ask guests to bring desserts, while family or friends prepare the main course

*   You could have the event catered

*   You may want to cook something yourself – a special food dish could be an aspect of your challenge.

After the ritual, you may want to have some games with your friends and family (it is a good idea to let go of the serious mood of the ritual with some silliness, some laughter), or you may want the rest of the celebration to be for visiting, dancing, and eating. Have the music as you wish, considering the whole group and its tastes. Have it all as you wish – have your passage into womanhood be perfectly wonderful!

Expressing your new responsibility, you certainly will want to help with the clean-up.

YOUR RITUAL

"The human spirit loves rituals.
Rituals connect us to wonder,
to self-discovery,
to the world of myths and symbols...
Rituals help us live our lives
more consciously.
Most importantly,
rituals provide a way
to connect us to our spirits."

Jennifer Louden, TV writer, and women's workshop leader

Generally, the ritual should be held at the beginning of the whole celebration when people are most prepared to focus on the serious meaning of your passage. The ritual gives form to your passage into womanhood and makes it visible. With this in mind, the beginning will be the formal or ceremonial part of the celebration.

The following are ideas for a ritual that you can adapt to your own unique expression. As people arrive:

* You could make a place of honor for an elder woman – your grandmother, a great aunt, or an older woman who is special to you in some way.

* Your mentors might welcome everyone and ask your guests to sit for your presentation.

* You then, could present your gifts and/or talents that you have prepared from the challenge you set for yourself.

* Your mentor/mentors could read a poem that refers to passing through an opening; for example, from *The Book of Runes*, the rune of "The Gateway" reads:

"Visualize yourself standing before a gateway on a hilltop.
Your entire life lies out behind you and below.
Before you step through, pause and review the past:
the learning and the joys, the victories and the sorrows –
everything it took to bring you here.
Observe it all, bless it all, release it all.
For in letting go of the past you reclaim your power.
Step through the Gateway now. "

* It's your moment – you could step, dance, or jump through your Gateway, your way into womanhood!!

* You could have someone place a wreath upon your head, or your mentors may want to surprise you with something to make this moment truly special. It is your moment of triumph! You have presented and defined yourself as a young woman. At this time, you may want to say your name to the circle and have them say a welcome to you out loud. They might sing your name back to you. This also confirms your moment of entry.

* It is the moment for your guests to honor you. Perhaps here, you would like to serve some juice for the "toasting" during which you, or your mentors could invite others to offer a song, a poem, a story of their experiences, or a pledge of support to you within the circle. Receiving applause and compliments can be surprisingly stressful – or it may be the easiest moment for you. In either case, remember that you have chosen to be here, and from *the way of courage*, you will be able to meet what comes. So much goodness may come that you may have to remind yourself to breathe! Breathe it all in, knowing that you have earned the love you see reflected towards you.

What I have offered are merely suggestions. To make the ritual your own, you will envision how you see your ritual unfolding. Share your ideas with your mentors and be open to their thoughts. They may already have experience with staging events – attending to such details as where in the room you will give your presentation, where your audience will sit, and where the lighting is best (perhaps you will want to have a videographer record your event). As you bring your ideas and skills together, you will be able to create a ritual that will feel just right.

Symbols

Here are some physical things that you can use to represent the passage from childhood to womanhood:

bowl: A vessel or container usually circular to represent the womb, the feminine.

candles: Represent clarity, light, purification, and blessing. A candle or many candles change the atmosphere of a place and make a room feel serene and special. They bring delight.

circle: The oldest symbol of humankind is the circle, without beginning without end. It represents wholeness and in this context, the unending cycle of grandmother, mother, daughter.

color: Since the event of becoming a woman also indicates that you have, or soon will be getting your menstrual periods, you may want to celebrate this with use of the color red – either wearing red, or wearing white and carrying red flowers. You may feel like wearing a special dress or just an everyday outfit, or you may ask everyone to wear a specific color or type of clothing.

flowers: Symbolizing your feminine beauty. Flowers can be used to decorate the room, your hair and your gateway. The word 'flow' resides within the word flower, and we women are indeed "flow-ers" – our bodies flow with monthly blood, we are likely to wear flowing garments (at least now and then) and we are flowing as we change in our roles and relationships. Roses, in particular, symbolize love, and may be used in a bouquet, or as petals on the floor in a designated area. The rose is considered the most exquisite, delicate and many faceted (faced) of all the flowers.

rope: To symbolize your connection to your mother, you could arrange to be tied together with a rope or cord. Your mother could lead you into your community of girls and women, cutting or untying the rope from you to symbolize your new position as a separate young woman.

water: Represents purification. It can add a beautiful element to your ceremony, cleansing you from your past, and preparing you for your future. Pure water from nature could be drawn from a well, a brook, the sea or from rainwater. You might ask your mentor or your mother to dab your face with water, or bathe and oil your feet. Flowers could be used in the water if you choose.

I hope you are getting the idea that certain objects are already imbued with cultural meaning, but that the choice is always yours to include what has meaning for you.

Congratulations

"Flower and even fruit are only the beginning.
In the seed lies the life and the future."
Marion Zimmer Bradley, historical novelist

Your hard work has born fruit. You have marked your place in the cycle of womanhood. You have celebrated who you have become and who you are becoming. Congratulations! It is completely natural to feel a sense of pride and completion for what you have accomplished.

Now that you know how to create your own ritual, you can mark many events intuitively and creatively; for example, the entrance of a pet into your family, the death of a pet, the moving away of a friend, or the development of a new friendship. You can use your new understanding of celebrations to enhance holidays and birthdays – your own and those of your family and friends.

You can be the one who encourages others to establish intention in their lives by making ceremonies. The stories you will have to tell of your own experiences will encourage others and give them ideas. This circle that you have created, and other circles like it, can be a source to which you give, and from which you receive love and support throughout your life. The individuals comprising your circle will probably change, but you will have established a form and a value that can be recreated wherever you are.

I hope that you will keep this book as a reference when you plan future celebrations. You may wish to keep your notes, photos, and cards from your celebration in a scrapbook, or in the pages at the back of this book.

Words of Thanks

"How we receive a gift can be a gift to the giver...
Accepting other people's generosity is a form of generosity."
Sue Bender, author, artist, and lecturer

Now that your celebration is over, you may be feeling more "adult", more responsible. Wonderful! On the strength of this new feeling, you could take time to appreciate the presents that you have received from the women in your circle. Honor the givers with thoughts about what their gifts mean to you. In this way, you are completing the circle and closing the ritual with awareness.

Your mentors have given an immeasurable gift to you. It is up to you (or perhaps you and your mother) to decide how to thank them.

GLOSSARY

adolescence: the state or process of growing up – usually occurring between the ages of 11 and 18.

celebration: an act of performing publicly and according to rule or form; to honor someone or something with special activities or festivities.

ceremony: a formal act or series of acts prescribed by ritual or custom.

a challenge: something that requires full use of one's talents or abilities.

creation: the act of creating – of bringing something new into existence.

creative ability: the ability to confront and deal with a problem, resourcefulness.

gateway: a gateway is a place of transition, a threshold or doorway that takes one from one way of being to an altogether new. A gateway can be anything to represent stepping through from one side to another.

gift: in this case, gift refers to the unique talents, skills, or interests that your being alive, bring to your community.

intuition: something known or understood at once without an effort of the mind.

a rite: a specified form for a ceremony.

ritual: "a drama that communicates our deepest values... and inscribes order in the hearts and minds of participants". (The Circle of Life, David Cohen)

symbol: an icon or image that stands for something else; for example, the candle represents light.

toast: a ritual that involves a speech, or drink in honor of another person.

Resources

The following are only a few of the wonderful books available. I hope you become as informed as you can be about the changes that are happening in your lives.

Books:
Mindy Bingham, Judy Edmondson and Sandy Stryker, *Choices: A Teen Woman's Journal for Self-awareness and Personal Planning*, Advocacy Press, Santa Barbara, California, 1985, updated in 1993.

Patty Ellis, *Girl Power, Making Choices and Taking Control*, Momentum Book, Ltd. 6964 Crooks Road, Troy, Michigan, 1994.

Monica Furlong, *Wise Child*, Alfred A. Knopf, New York, New York, 1987.

Monica Furlong, *Juniper*, Alfred A. Knopf, New York, New York, 1990.

Emily Hancock, *The Girl Within*, Fawcett Columbine, New York, New York, 1989.

Mavis Jukes, *Growing Up, It's A Girl Thing: Straight Talk About First Bras, First Periods, and Your Changing Body*, Alfred A. Knopf, New York, New York, 1998.

Francis A. Karnes and Suzanne M. Bean, *Girls and Young Women Leading the Way: Twenty True Stories About Leadership*, MInneapolis Free Spirit Publishing, Minneapolis, MN, 1993.

Lynda Madaras, *My Feelings, My Self: A Growing up Guide For Girls*, New Market Press, 18 East 48th Street, New York, New York, 10017.

Gertrude Mueller Nelson, *Here All Dwell Free: Stories to Heal the Wounded Feminine*, Ballantine Books, New York, New York, 1991.

Websites:
http://www.talentdevelop.com/books-t.html
http://www.shykids.com/shykidsbooksteens.htm

NOTES

NOTES

NOTES

NOTES

NOTES

NOTES

NOTES

NOTES

Photos

PHOTOS

PHOTOS

PHOTOS

PHOTOS

PHOTOS

Photos

Photos

PHOTOS

PHOTOS

Frederica Chapman, M.S., is a mother of 5 children, a performance artist, theatre director, and healer. She is founder/director of *Veronica Institute*, *Arts For The Earth*, a non-profit organization, and Director of *Theatre For The Earth*, a professional touring company of women that performs internationally for schools, conferences, and cathedrals. *Theatre for the Earth* offers a workshop entitled, "The Gateway Rite of Passage Workshop for Girls, Women, and Elder Women" in which girls' rites of passage, and the strength between the generations of women are celebrated. Out of the work of *Theatre For The Earth*, Frederica has written and published, "The Princess Who Greened The Land: A Fairy Tale For The 21st Century". Frederica holds a Master's degree in Mental Health Nursing, and works with women's groups, and sound healing in her counseling practice in Portland, Maine.

To arrange a Workshop for your group, contact Frederica at info@VeronicaInstitute.org